SIMPLE LAWS OF ATTENTION

By

EDEN WILSON

Table of Contents

Introduction

It is crucial that you familiarize yourself with the concept of the "law of attraction," or LOA, if you are going through a difficult moment in your life. According to the law of attraction, you are largely to blame for all the conditions both the good and the terrible, of your life. Everything that you desire comes to you. You have the ability to influence your life to go in a good direction Just need to understand how to use the law of attraction's power

Every aspect of your existence is affected by the law of attraction. Everything you do, including your thoughts, feelings, and actions, either increases or decreases this power. If I told you that it is, do you think you'd believe me? Is it possible for you to realize all of your goals and experience true happiness in life? It's true, and it's also a lot easier than you probably realize. All you possess to act, one must have faith in the world and harness the force of the law of attraction, and your efforts will undoubtedly be rewarded. It is crucial to keep in mind that change almost probably won't happen overnight. Before the law of attraction takes full effect, it will probably take some time. Your life will start to come together the minute you fully comprehend and start applying the law of attraction. Everything will start to make more sense as the puzzle pieces start to fit better.

The law of attraction will be covered in more detail and explained in more detail in the future chapters of this book.

Chapter 1

When discussing the law of attraction, there are a few fundamental ideas that must be grasped. In essence, everything that occurs in your life is drawn to you, as was previously said. It's critical that you recognize and accept responsibility for the reality that everything that occurs in your life has a direct correlation to the choices or ideas you make. Imagine yourself as a large magnet to help you comprehend the law of attraction. Everything else in the world is now made up of magnet-attracted items. It's crucial that you are aware of the things you should avoid and the kinds of ideas you should strive to avoid thinking.

Even if you don't express an idea, it still has the power to bring certain things into your life. It's crucial that you develop cognitive skills and make an effort to think positively. The law of attraction has the power to change your life dramatically. You just must utilize it properly and have a thorough grasp of it. One
The fact that even if you do not apply the law is crucial to keep in mind
It still remains and is constantly in operation to your benefit, even if adversely. Therefore, you may as well seize it and realize its full potential.
of its strength.

The fundamentals of the law of attraction will be covered in the subsequent chapter so that

You'll be able to comprehend what it really is better. The law of attraction is responsible for everything that occurs in life. In essence, anything you thought about, decided to do, or did is what caused everything to play out the way it does. Things move in a large circle, yet they always end up back where they started. Therefore, if you act or think positively, positive things will ultimately come your way. On the other side, if you act negatively and have unpleasant emotions, nothing but negativity will return to you. The law of attraction cannot be avoided or avoided. It really has an impact on all aspect of our life. The law of attraction is responsible for everything, including the fact that I am writing this book and that you are reading it. There are several individuals nowadays who doubt the efficacy of attraction. They consider everything that occurs in their lives to be pure luck of the card hand that was given to them. Most of the time, these individuals' lives are out of control or are disintegrating in the process. Living life without following the guidelines of the law of attraction is like operating a vehicle without a steering wheel and trying to arrive at your intended destination without encountering any negative events en route to the objective.

Thoughts are valid, and so is the notion that you should not allow anything into your life there. The law of attraction is heavily influenced by the lessons we all learned as children. Every action we take has a reaction, as we were told, and thus nothing could be more accurate. Everything we do has a knock-on effect, which prompts something else to occur, and so forth until it comes to a conclusion. back into your lap straight now. Do you want it to be good or negative when it comes around again? You undoubtedly want it to be favorable. You must trust in the power of the universe and act positively if you want to get good things from the cosmos.

Chapter 2

Learning the skill of meditation can have a variety of positive effects. Meditating is not only great for your health and for reducing stress, but it can also be highly helpful for using the law of attraction. You can block out the outside world while meditating and to establish a really strong connection with oneself. You'll have access to hearing when you pause to reflect, many things come to mind, including your innermost wishes. It will start to make sense in your life. Everything you do affects how the law of attraction will function in your life, as was previously explained. Up to and including the ideas you have, this is accurate. Although it is true that actions will have a greater influence than ideas under the law of attraction, thoughts still matter.

Using meditation as a technique can help you gain control over your ideas and start to completely alter how you think.

The many advantages of mastering the practice of meditation are covered in the chapter that follows. You'll get some advice on how to meditate more effectively. We will also discuss the connection between meditation and the law of attraction.

Use meditation

Learning the right way to mediate and regularly using this ability can have a variety of positive effects. The benefits of meditation and how closely it relates to the law of attraction are not widely known. It's real, and you won't fully comprehend it until you go through it.

The various advantages that the practice of meditation may bring about include the following.

- **Relaxation via meditation**

The practice of meditation is an excellent approach to lower your stress levels.

When trying to reduce your stress levels, it is highly helpful to learn how to shut off the outer world and concentrate on yourself.

When under a lot of stress, we may behave aggressively or irritably, which are not typical behaviors for us. As previously said, the law of attraction is influenced by everything you do in life, including your ideas and attitudes. You must thus find a strategy to reduce your stress levels, and meditation is unquestionably one of them.

- **Meditation Aids Us in Discovering Our True Selves**

Simply put, your body serves as a temple for your actual self. Self must discover who the true you is if you want the law of attraction to operate in your favor. You'll need to have the ability to peek underneath your outer shell and discover your true self. Your spirit and intellect are where the real you resides, not in the body that serves just as a barrier. You can turn off the outer world and all of its distractions by meditating. You'll be able to use this to reflect on your true identity and life goals.

- **Meditation Aids in Emotional Coping**

A person may benefit much from meditation when it comes to managing and coping with their emotions, among many other things. In life, things might happen that leave us feeling sad or melancholy.

By using the power of the law of attraction, continuing down this road of negative emotions will only result in more negative outcomes in your life. People who master the practice of meditation will get a greater understanding of and ability to manage their emotions. They will be able to see the better things in life when they have better emotional control, and the law of attraction will then cause more good things to come into their lives.

- **Meditation Aids in Personal Improvement**

Learning the art of meditation will make you a more complete person. Although the results won't be felt right away, over time you'll undoubtedly notice the improvements and differences in your life. The law of attraction will favor you as you improve as a person. The law of attraction may be visualized as a large circle, where good things will circle back around to you if you put good into it, as was previously covered in this book. You will undoubtedly be contributing a lot more positive things to this circle if you improve yourself, so you will receive a tremendous number of positive things in return. Meditation may genuinely benefit your life in this way.

- **Even if you're not meditating, it still works.**

One of the nicest things about meditation is that you will continue to experience its benefits even when you are not actively practicing it. You'll see that the minor inconveniences that used to cause you a lot of anxiety have diminished in importance. You will learn to constantly look on the bright side of things and to believe in the cosmos, which will improve your ability to deal with issues in your life. These items together will help the law of attraction bring benefits into your life.

The advantages of meditation range widely, and the ones listed above are only a few of them. There are many more, but discussing them would take all day. The law of attraction and meditation are closely related, therefore if you wish to use the power of attraction working in your favor You will need to develop these skills to grasp this ability. You'll need to develop the ability to tune out the outside world and put your attention on your relationship to the cosmos and your genuine self.

Chapter 3

Depending on your everyday choices, thoughts, and feelings, the law of attraction is a tremendously potent force that will continue to draw both good and terrible things into your life. You want to make sure that you are drawing as much good energy as you can and as little bad energy as you can from the cosmos.

You must learn to regulate the law of attraction in order to attract only positive things into your life because, as previously indicated, it cannot be stopped or avoided. The last thing you want is for things to be going well and then something enters your life that completely derails everything.

It will take time, patience, and work to figure out how to harness the law of attraction to your advantage, but the effort will be well worth it in the end. When you comprehend LOA and put it to good use, you'll be astounded at how wonderful your life becomes.

The importance of attracting the proper things into your life will be discussed in the next chapter, which will also provide you some tips on how to start attracting more good things. Keep in mind that you will need to learn how to do this, and you might not be able to do it right away.

Your inner self emits energy into the cosmos that resembles radio signals in some ways. These signs include your wants, ideas, and these messages will be picked up on by your activities and the law of attraction. As was said previously, the law of attraction is influenced by everything in your life. You may utilize this ability to attract a wealth of favorable circumstances and chances to enter your life. Make sure you're consistently sending out constructive cues to notice the law of attraction. The law of attraction will bring into your life what you project that you want. The thing is, sometimes we project signals without even knowing we are doing so. It's critical that we connect with and figure out how to speak with our actual inner selves.

We must develop emotional and mental self-control. In what Our thoughts have an impact on how we behave and the things that we do daily activities. Therefore, it's crucial that we look for opportunities to start thinking more rationally so that we may make better decisions. The law of attraction will favor your activities. Other factors, such as the environment, can also have an impact on the law of attraction of friends you may have in your life or persons you choose to be friends with whom you are affiliated with.

You will be affected by bad energy if you choose to be around negative individuals. The law of attraction will be activated by this negative energy, and you will start to unintentionally draw bad things into your life. You'll quickly realize that everything is getting out of hand and that only bad things are happening to you. However, if you are surrounded by wonderful individuals who radiate positive energy, you will Enjoy the benefits of the law of attraction as you start to draw more uplifting things into your life. What you want the law of attraction to bring into your life is ultimately up to you to decide. Consider the proof for this law's existence that is all around us if you still find it difficult to believe how strong it is. If you think about it, every action has a reaction, therefore be sure your acts are good and will result in good results.

Chapter 4

If you know how to ask for what you want, the universe is tremendously strong and can provide you the finest life imaginable. Many individuals are not aware of the advantages of asking the cosmos for what they desire. However, some individuals are aware of the power of the universe but are unable to fully access their inner selves in order to choose what they truly desire.

You must have a solid grasp of how to communicate with the universe and how to ask it for what you want in order to effectively use the law of attraction. Keep in mind that you are not supposed to expect results right away when doing this. You must have confidence in the cosmos and demonstrate your trust in it for it to be kind to you. By doing this, the law of attraction will reward your confidence and rewards will undoubtedly enter your life, even if they come in the form of a disguised blessing. The significance of the universe will be discussed in the next chapter, along with how the law of attraction and asking the universe for what you desire are related.

Request the things you really want.

When you make a request to the universe, you are actually starting the process. The law of attraction will help us get what we desire out of life just to request it. You must, however, conduct your life in a way that is moral. No matter who you ask, you won't get what you want. The speed at which everything you need arrives will astound you. When you make the request, everything you've ever wanted starts to work for it. Everything starts to come to pass, and your life starts to attain genuine blessings.

As long as you are willing, all of the tools and motivation you need to achieve everything in your life that you have ever desired will start to arrive into your life.

When you talk to the cosmos, be sincere. If you don't know what you want, you won't be able to ask the universe for it. Be certain about your goals. This is where practices like meditation and other internal self-communication are involved. You must be able to see closely. Find out what your genuine desires are by looking within. You must be able to block out all other influences and figure out what it is you really desire rather than what else. Asking the world for what you want will be a lot simpler if you can interact with your inner self and discover what your actual wishes are. Make sure in order to ensure that you get what you desire from the universe the fact that you are quite clear about what you desire. You must not be evasive and you can't omit any information. There is no such thing as mind reading and it's crucial that you do so if you want it to grant you what you want. You express your desires clearly to the object.

The cosmos and the law of attraction can bestow many blessings upon you. Finding out what your inner self truly wants from life and what you want to ask the universe for is all that is required. Everything is attainable if you put your mind to it.

Chapter 5

When attempting to employ the law of attraction to attract wonderful things into your life, writing affirmations may be quite helpful. Believe it or not, merely speaking or writing positive affirmations may have a profoundly good effect on your life. You will begin to believe them and they will come true once you have said or written enough encouraging things about the blessings you wish to experience in your life.

As was previously mentioned, your mindset affects the law of attraction. As a result, if you have positive thinking that is strengthened by the power of affirmations, the law of attraction will begin to bring good things into your life quickly. You will be astounded by the results. The significance of writing affirmations and the reasons why they are so crucial when attempting to take advantage of the law of attraction are covered in the chapter that follows. Additionally, we'll discuss how to create powerful affirmations that really work.

It is crucial for you to make sure that you are writing your affirmations in a certain way if you want them to be helpful. The step-by-step steps that follow should make it easier for you to compose the most potent affirmation.

- Start by writing a string of I am statements. This is one of the simplest ways to begin writing affirmations.

These declarations should be about who or what you wish to become or bring into your life. Doesn't this sound incredibly easy to understand? That is due to how easy it is. The law of attraction may start to make these words true by doing something as basic as writing them out every day. You must always keep in mind to trust these assertions, or otherwise the entire procedure would be a waste of time. Although initially finding these claims credible may be challenging, with time it will become lot easier.

- It's crucial to avoid writing any negative thoughts when writing your affirmations. You want to keep things upbeat. Therefore, you should pay attention to details like what you wish to bring in, not what you want to get out of it, but your life. The power of magnetism will respond to what you believe and write, so any negative remarks might have unintended consequences.

- It's crucial to be authentically you at all times in life. Never attempt to be someone other than who you truly are. Even when you discuss how you write your affirmations out, this is accurate. You want to utilize language that comes naturally to you. Avoid attempting to sound distinct. It is accurate to say that you are genuine to who you are and that you are honest with yourself.

- It is vitally crucial that you write your affirmations out with a lot of enthusiasm and vigor. You want to infuse them with a little of your individuality. If you make them boring and uninteresting, they will appear more like a task than an affirmation. Spend some time creating affirmations since they should be joyful and inspiring.

- You should avoid wasting time wondering about how your affirmations will materialize. The law of attraction is in charge of doing that. You will attract such things into your life when you write down your affirmations and sincerely believe them. As previously indicated, it might not occur immediately, but sooner or later it will.

I promise you'll be astonished by the strength of affirmations; all you have to do is give it a go to see for yourself. Positive affirmations are a great way to harness the power of the law of attraction and use it to your advantage. The law of attraction is very strong.

Chapter 6

It is crucial that you acknowledge and believe that you already have a lot in life if you want to use the law of attraction to your advantage. You must learn to be appreciative of what the universe has given you and to constantly remember that there are individuals in this world who have far more than you have.
You'll also see that you're gifted with a sense of tranquility and contentment when you start to feel appreciative for what you have and that you have enough in your life.

You'll also see that the law of attraction will shower you with nice things in your life when you are thankful for what you have and believe that you have enough in life. You should demonstrate gratitude as much as you can since it will positively affect the law of attraction. The significance of appreciating what you have and how it relates to the law of attraction will be discussed in the chapter that follows.

Many individuals attempt to live their lives in a way that will lead the law of attraction to bring positive things into their lives because they are aware of its power. Funny thing is, they frequently skip one of the most crucial and straightforward steps in utilizing the law of attraction to their advantage. This is the stage where you remember to feel thankful and abundantly blessed. This is crucial because the universe will not reward people who it perceives as self-centered and those who lack gratitude for its favors. Even individuals who are aware of this attraction awareness phase nevertheless decide to ignore it, and this never leads to a good result.

Every area of a person's life may be transformed by gratitude almost immediately.

Practicing gratitude as often as you can is a very effective law of attraction activity. Your frequency will rise as a result of this activity, which will put you into harmony with the cosmos.

Different sorts of people will come into your life on a daily basis. You will observe that folks that appear fortunate have a lot of wonderful things in their lives, like happiness, a fine automobile, a lovely house, and money. They are appreciative of what they have, which is something else you'll notice.

On the other hand, those who appear unhappy and do not have much in life share a common trait: none of them express gratitude for what they have. You must always be grateful for what you have because, as previously said, the universe will not reward those who are ungrateful or selfish. A person just has to identify one item for which to be grateful in their life, regardless of how miserable their circumstances may be.

for. Even in difficult circumstances, being grateful will be seen by the universe, and the

law of attraction will reward you for your thankfulness.
Complaining will just make your life more difficult. Complaining indicates that you believe there is a wrong with something that the universe is through. The cosmos is aware that there are no difficulties, which is the problem with this. Everything occurs for a purpose, and the cosmos is aware of this. It also understands that the law of attraction applies to everything that occurs in your life and that everything is a product of your own deeds, thoughts, or emotions.

You actually have no idea if you believe your life would be difficult right now. All you need to do is whine as much as you can if you want to lose all you now own. The cosmos doesn't applaud those who whine about their circumstances and doing so will bring nothing but unfavorable outcomes. Anything you want in life is genuinely attainable. All you need to do is have faith in what both the cosmos and its purpose is for you. You'll find yourself in the same situation regardless of the route you pick in life.

The most crucial thing is that you choose to go down the easy route, which is paved with riches, happiness, and other benefits, as opposed to the difficult road, which is paved with disappointments and difficult times. The secret to choosing the easy path is to constantly be thankful to the universe and to use every chance to express how much you value what you have. If you follow this strategy, you will undoubtedly experience blessings at some point in the future.

www.ingramcontent.com/pod-product-compliance
Lightning Source LLC
LaVergne TN
LVHW020533160826
845677LV00015B/4037